Where Bat Came From

A Creek Tale

retold by Sharon Fear
illustrated by Lisa Desimini

Scott Foresman

Editorial Offices: Glenview, Illinois • New York, New York
Sales Offices: Reading, Massachusetts • Duluth, Georgia
Glenview, Illinois • Carrollton, Texas • Menlo Park, California

Mouse plays ball.

He plays with every friend.

They can kick.

Mouse can not.

They can run.

Mouse can not.

They can catch.

Mouse can not!

Mouse is sad.

"Jump!" said Mother Mouse.

Mouse can jump.

"Jump!" said Mother Mouse.

"Again!" said Mother Mouse.

Mouse jumps and jumps.
Up and up and up!

One day he jumps up.
And Mouse can fly!
Every friend looks.

Now Mouse is not sad.

Now Mouse is not Mouse!

Mouse is Bat!

Bat plays ball.

He can do it!